The perfect start to your day

Brunch

The perfect start to your day

Brunch

Simone Lloyd

BARNES & NOBLE

NEW YORK

Cover and internal design by Talking Design.
Introduction by Linda Doeser.

2006 Barnes & Noble Publishing

ISBN - 13: 987-0-7607-8486-0
ISBN - 10: 0-7607-8486-8

Printed and bound in China

1 3 5 7 9 10 8 6 4 2

NOTES FOR READER

This book uses imperial, metric or US cup measurements. Follow the same units of measurements throughout, do not mix imperial and metric. All spoon measurements are level: teaspoons are assumed to be 5ml, and tablespoons are assumed to be 15ml. Unless otherwise stated, milk is assumed to be low fat and eggs are medium. The times given are an approximate guide only.

Some recipes contain nuts. If you are allergic to nuts you should avoid using them and any products containing nuts. Recipes using raw or very lightly cooked eggs should be avoided by infants, the elderly, pregnant women, convalescents and anyone suffering from illness.

CONTENTS

INTRODUCTION

Brunch does exactly what it says—it's a meal that combines breakfast and lunch. It wasn't really invented, but evolved almost spontaneously quite early in the last century as a means of informal entertaining on the weekend.

Americans are known for their hospitality, enthusiasm, energy, and ingenuity and the institution of brunch encapsulates all these qualities. Leisure time was—and still is—precious, but so are friends and family. Formal entertaining is delightful, but hard work, quite nerve-racking even for an experienced cook, and often expensive. Little time is then left on the weekend for other leisure activities—until people started having brunch.

Family brunch and brunch parties have long been immensely popular throughout the United States and eventually the British and other English-speaking nations began to appreciate the idea, yet it hasn't really caught on in most other parts of the world. Perhaps there is a shared Anglophone memory of what the British used to call "elevenses"—a mid-morning snack eaten with a cup of coffee some hours after breakfast and a couple of hours before lunch.

When is brunch?

It is, perhaps, ironic that the nation that invented brunch also invented early morning breakfast meetings—but then they take place during the week. Brunch definitely does not start at the crack of dawn. The keynote is relaxation so the idea is to let everyone, including yourself, make a leisurely start to the day. However, it does need to start during the morning, as people will be hungry and, by midday, they will be expecting a different kind of meal all together. It is logical that somewhere between 10 and 11 o'clock is a good choice for starting brunch.

However, no meal is more flexible than brunch so it is easy to adapt the timing to suit your specific plans for the day or just to your general lifestyle. An earlier brunch, with more emphasis on coffee, eggs, and pancakes and less on cocktails, salads, and pastries, is ideal before a family outing or a mass exodus of guests to the local game. The opposite is a better choice if you want more preparation time and like your guests to linger on in the afternoon.

The successful brunch party

As the essence of brunch is that it is a combination of two meals, try to plan the menu so that it incorporates both typical breakfast- and lunch-style dishes. However, you will not want to spend the entire time in the kitchen producing an endless succession of freshly cooked food with no opportunity to talk to your friends. If you browse through the recipes in this book, you can mix and match a selection of hot and cold food and choose some dishes that can be cooked in advance, some

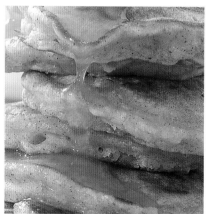

that can be prepared ready for cooking, and ones to cook from scratch during the morning. This is particularly important because, just as with barbecues, brunches tempt people's appetites and they tend to eat far more than they—or you—expected.

Variety is also a characteristic of brunch menus. When you make your selection of recipes, try to choose a mix of different types of dishes. So if you want to serve pancakes, don't cook blinis as well, and avoid duplicating dishes with the same main ingredient. Create a mix of fresh-tasting, spicy, richly flavored, and plainer dishes. If you have any vegetarian guests, make sure that you have catered to their needs. Brunch is also an occasion when there is likely to be quite a large mix of adults and children, so keep the tastes of the younger generation in mind too.

Serve the breakfast-style dishes first. Rolls, croissants, fruit muffins, granola, and compotes can be placed on the table before guests arrive. You can buy some of these ready-made, but there are some fabulous recipes in this book for preparing them yourself. Have all your ingredients and pans ready for any hot dishes you intend to serve, and cook them at spaced intervals. Not only will this give you time to spend with your guests, but it will let them pace their consumption. You don't want to give everybody indigestion. Add extra cold dishes, as well as extra rolls if necessary, from time to time during the course of the morning.

Obviously the amount of food you serve depends on the number of guests invited. You can easily add to the choice without creating lots of extra work for yourself. For example, a bowl of fresh strawberries or a tray of melon slices is always welcome, supermarkets these days offer a wide range of different breads and rolls, and a platter of cold meats is a perfect choice for brunch.

Everyone will want a drink but what they want will probably change during the course of the morning. Fresh coffee is a must throughout and a choice of fruit juice will be appreciated by both adults and children. Later, you may want to serve wine or beer and, perhaps, sodas for children, drivers, and non-drinkers. If you would like to make some drinks yourself, look no further than the third chapter of this book, where you will find fabulous fruit smoothies, refreshing coolers, and classic cocktails.

Don't forget all those important extras, such as cream, milk, sugar, and, if you're really thoughtful, sweetener, for coffee, cereal, and fruit. Make sure that there's plenty of butter (and, maybe, low-fat

Of course, brunch doesn't have to involve guests, fun though it is to throw a brunch party.

spread) for bread and rolls and you might also like to include dishes of marmalade and fruit jams. People will probably require salt and pepper for savory dishes, and providing other condiments—ketchup, Worcestershire sauce, and mustard—would also be considerate.

If this all sounds a little daunting, you can take comfort from another similarity between the barbecue and the brunch. Both generate a powerful feel-good factor that makes guests eager to help. Even members of the family will often assist with good will rather than grudgingly. Don't turn down offers to clear plates, stack the dishwasher, hand round fresh dishes of food, or make another pot of coffee. A brunch party should be as enjoyable and—almost—as relaxing for you as it is for your guests.

Family brunch

Of course, brunch doesn't have to involve guests, fun though it is to throw a brunch party. It is a great way for families to spend precious time together and catch up on everything that has been happening in each other's lives during the week. Make Sunday morning a lazy time, cook a couple of special brunch treats, and enjoy an informal meal together. This is an especially good way to touch base with teenagers, who never want to get out of bed early and rebel against more formal family meals, although younger kids enjoy the relaxed atmosphere too.

The leisurely mood of brunch gives everyone a chance to wind down and good food makes people feel good—not just about themselves, but also about others. Sibling rivalry will be banished and both generations may well find themselves talking to each other with an unfamiliar ease. Brunch is a great way to cement family relations, especially if dad takes over at the stove for some of the time and gives mom a break.

Friends' brunch

Life isn't like television and sometimes it is hard to keep in touch with old friends when we have just started new careers, moved to new homes, are constantly meeting new people, and are leading frantically busy lives. By getting together for brunch, you can meet up again and enjoy yourselves without the expense of restaurants, the hassle of cooking a formal meal yourself, the risk of disturbing other people with excited laughter and gossip, or taking time out from all the new and demanding things in your life.

If one person acts as host and everybody provides the food, you have the makings of a terrific occasion without any one of you doing too much work or spending too much money. Everyone must provide one dish—either home-cooked and ready to eat or the ingredients and willingness to prepare it when you get to the host's apartment. It is a good idea for the host to make a list of the types of dishes, so that everyone brings something different and complementary. There is no need to be too serious, though, and it is important to avoid turning a fun sharing experience into a major task. When everyone makes a little effort, this is all about contributing, not competing; sharing the workload, not aiming to be the best. All the recipes in this book are easy to follow and most are well within the scope of inexperienced cooks. If you really want to show how delighted you are with the reunion, make a smoothie or even a cocktail as well.

You will have a lovely morning with edible surprises and plenty of time to chat, recall old times, and talk about new events. As brunch is all about leisure and informality, you can be sure that there will be none of those awkward silences that sometimes happen when you get together with friends you haven't seen for a while. Just unpacking your offerings and cooking your dishes is sure to break the ice and get the conversation going. It's one of those times when you can be all girls together or a mixed group without any pressures and, if you have to leave before the others, you won't break up the party. Ideally, of course, you should all stay long enough to clear things away and wash the dishes or stack the dishwasher. Next time, another one of your group can act as host.

The Classic Brunch

EGGS BENEDICT WITH QUICK HOLLANDAISE SAUCE

For best results when poaching eggs, break them into a cup first, then slide them into the hot water. Poach for a little longer than the suggested three minutes if you prefer firmer yolks.

INGREDIENTS

1 tbsp white wine vinegar

4 eggs

4 English muffins

4 slices good-quality ham

QUICK HOLLANDAISE SAUCE

3 egg yolks

1¾ sticks butter

1 tbsp lemon juice

pepper

SERVES 4

Fill a wide skillet three-quarters full with water and bring to a boil over low heat. Reduce the heat to a simmer and add the vinegar. When the water is barely shimmering, carefully break the eggs into the skillet. Let stand for 1 minute, then, using a large spoon, gently loosen the eggs from the bottom of the skillet. Let cook for an additional 3 minutes, or until the white is cooked and the yolk is still soft, basting the top of the egg with the water from time to time.

Meanwhile, to make the hollandaise sauce, place the egg yolks in a blender or food processor. Melt the butter in a small pan until bubbling. With the motor running, gradually add the hot butter in a steady stream until the sauce is thick and creamy. Add the lemon juice, and a little warm water if the sauce is too thick, then season to taste with pepper. Remove from the blender or food processor and keep warm.

Split the muffins and toast them on both sides. To serve, top each muffin with a slice of ham, a poached egg, and a generous spoonful of hollandaise sauce.

EGGS FLORENTINE

INGREDIENTS

1 lb/450 g fresh spinach leaves, rinsed

½ stick sweet butter

2 oz/55 g white mushrooms, sliced

6 tbsp pine nuts

6 scallions, chopped

salt and pepper

4 eggs

scant ¼ cup whole-wheat flour

1¼ cups milk, warmed

1 tsp prepared English mustard

3 oz/85 g sharp Cheddar cheese, grated

SERVES 2–4

Preheat the oven to 375°F/190°C. Shake off any excess water from the spinach, put into a large pan over medium heat with only the water clinging to the leaves, and sprinkle with a little salt. Cover and cook for 2–3 minutes, or until wilted. Drain, pressing out any excess liquid, then chop.

Heat 1 tablespoon of the butter in a small pan over medium heat, add the mushrooms, and cook for 2 minutes, stirring frequently. Add the pine nuts and scallions and cook for an additional 2 minutes. Remove, season to taste with salt and pepper, and sprinkle over the spinach. Set aside.

Meanwhile, fill a skillet with cold water and bring to a boil, then reduce the heat to a gentle simmer. Carefully break an egg into a cup and slip into the water. Add the remaining eggs and cook for 4–5 minutes, or until set. Carefully remove with a slotted spoon and arrange on top of the spinach mixture.

Melt the remaining butter in a pan and stir in the flour. Cook for 2 minutes, then remove from the heat and gradually stir in the milk. Return to the heat and cook, stirring constantly, until the mixture comes to a boil and has thickened. Stir in the mustard, then 2 oz/55 g of the cheese. Continue stirring until the cheese has melted. Add salt and pepper to taste, then pour over the eggs, completely covering them. Sprinkle with the remaining cheese.

Cook in the preheated oven for 20–25 minutes, or until piping hot.

APPLE PANCAKES WITH MAPLE SYRUP BUTTER

As the batter sits, it tends to thicken up and can make the pancakes very doughy. If the mixture becomes too thick while you are cooking the pancakes, add a little extra milk before continuing.

INGREDIENTS

scant 1½ cups self-rising flour

½ cup superfine sugar

1 tsp ground cinnamon

1 egg

scant 1 cup milk

2 apples, peeled, cored, and grated

1 tsp butter

MAPLE SYRUP BUTTER

¾ stick butter, softened

3 tbsp maple syrup

2 whole strawberries, to garnish

MAKES 18 PANCAKES TO SERVE 4–6

Mix the flour, sugar, and cinnamon together in a bowl and make a well in the center. Beat the egg and milk together and pour into the well. Using a wooden spoon, gently incorporate the dry ingredients into the liquid until well combined, then stir in the grated apple.

Heat the butter in a large nonstick skillet over low heat until melted and bubbling. Add tablespoons of the pancake mixture to form 3½-inch/9-cm circles. Cook each pancake for about 1 minute, until it starts to bubble lightly on the top and looks set, then flip it over and cook the other side for 30 seconds, or until cooked through. The pancakes should be golden brown; if not, increase the heat a little. Remove from the skillet and keep warm. Repeat the process until all of the pancake batter has been used up (it is not necessary to add extra butter).

To make the maple syrup butter, melt the butter with the maple syrup in a pan over low heat and stir until combined. To serve, place the pancakes on serving dishes and spoon over the flavored butter. Serve warm, garnished with whole strawberries.

BUCKWHEAT CRÊPES WITH MAPLE SYRUP BANANAS

INGREDIENTS

generous ⅓ cup buckwheat flour

generous ⅓ cup all-purpose flour

pinch of salt

1 large egg, lightly beaten

½ cup milk

½ cup water

3 tbsp margarine

FOR THE MAPLE SYRUP BANANAS

3 tbsp margarine

2 tbsp maple syrup

2 bananas, thickly sliced diagonally

SERVES 4

Sift both types of flour and the salt into a mixing bowl. Make a well in the center and add the beaten egg, milk, and water. Using a balloon whisk, gradually mix the flour into the liquid ingredients, whisking well to get rid of any lumps, until you have a smooth batter.

Melt 2 tablespoons of the margarine in a small pan and stir it into the batter. Pour the batter into a pitcher, cover, and let rest for 30 minutes.

Melt half the remaining margarine in a medium-size skillet. When the skillet is hot, pour in enough batter to make a thin crêpe, swirling the skillet to make an even layer.

Cook one side until lightly browned, then, using a spatula, turn over and cook the other side. Slide onto a warmed plate and cover with foil while you cook the remaining crêpes, adding more margarine when needed.

To make the maple syrup bananas, wipe the skillet, add the margarine, and heat until melted. Stir in the maple syrup, then add the bananas and cook for 2–3 minutes, or until the bananas have just softened and the sauce has thickened and caramelized. To serve, fold the crêpes in half and then half again, then top with bananas.

TOASTED ENGLISH MUFFINS WITH HONEY-GLAZED BACON & EGGS

Glazing the bacon in this way gives it a lovely sweet flavor, but don't leave it over the heat for too long as the honey tends to burn very quickly. Use maple syrup in the same way for a slightly different flavor.

INGREDIENTS

6 rindless unsmoked bacon slices

1 tbsp honey

3 oz/85 g canned corn kernels, drained

2 small tomatoes, diced

1 tbsp chopped fresh parsley

salt and pepper

4 eggs

2 English muffins, split, toasted, and buttered

SERVES 2

Heat a nonstick skillet over medium heat. Lay the bacon slices in the skillet and cook until lightly browned, then turn and cook the other side.

Warm the honey slightly and brush each bacon slice lightly with it. Cook the bacon for an additional 1 minute or so until it takes on a slight glaze. Remove from the skillet and keep warm.

Mix the corn, diced tomatoes, and chopped parsley together and season to taste with salt and pepper. Fry, poach, or scramble the eggs, as you prefer.

Serve the honey-glazed bacon and eggs on buttered toasted English muffins, topped with a spoonful of the corn and tomato mixture.

BAKED EGGS WITH CREAM, SPINACH & PARMESAN

INGREDIENTS

2 tbsp butter, plus extra for greasing

scant 3 cups baby spinach

½ tsp freshly grated nutmeg

4 small eggs

¼ cup light cream

2 tbsp freshly grated Parmesan cheese

salt and pepper

SERVES 2

Preheat the oven to 325°F/160°C. Lightly grease 2 individual ceramic gratin dishes or similar.

Melt the butter in a large skillet over low heat and add the spinach. Cook for 1 minute, stirring with a wooden spoon until the spinach starts to wilt. Season with a little nutmeg, then divide between the prepared dishes.

Gently break 2 eggs into each dish. Pour the cream over them, and sprinkle with grated Parmesan, then season to taste with salt and pepper. Bake for 10 minutes, or until the whites of the eggs have set but the yolks remain runny. Serve at once.

As a variation, add some diced ham or smoked salmon to the cooked spinach. The quantity of baby spinach used in this recipe may seem a lot but it shrinks substantially as it cooks.

FRESH CROISSANTS

Start this recipe the night before. Make the dough and roll out the croissants, then brush with the glaze, cover with plastic wrap and refrigerate overnight. The next morning, let rise for 30–45 minutes, then proceed as per the recipe.

INGREDIENTS

1 lb 2 oz/500 g white bread flour, plus extra for rolling

scant ¼ cup superfine sugar

1 tsp salt

2 tsp rapid-rise dried yeast

1¼ cups milk, heated until just warm to the touch

2 sticks plus 5 tbsp butter, softened, plus extra for greasing

1 egg, lightly beaten with 1 tbsp milk, for glazing

MAKES 12 CROISSANTS

Preheat the oven to 400°F/200°C. Stir the dry ingredients into a large bowl, make a well in the center, and add the milk. Mix to a soft dough, adding more milk if too dry. Knead on a lightly floured counter for 5–10 minutes, or until smooth and elastic. Let rise in a large greased bowl, covered, in a warm place until doubled in size. Meanwhile, flatten the butter with a rolling pin between two sheets of waxed paper to form a rectangle about ¼ inch/ 5 mm thick, then let chill.

Knead the dough for 1 minute. Remove the butter from the refrigerator and let soften slightly. Roll out the dough on a well-floured counter to 18 x 6 inches/ 45 x 15 cm. Place the butter in the center, folding up the sides and squeezing the edges together gently. With the short end of the dough toward you, fold the top third down toward the center, then fold the bottom third up. Rotate 90 degrees clockwise so that the fold is to your left and the top flap toward your right. Roll out to a rectangle and fold again. If the butter feels soft, wrap the dough in plastic wrap, and let chill. Repeat the rolling process twice more. Cut the dough in half. Roll out one half into a triangle ¼ inch/5 mm thick (keep the other half refrigerated). Use a cardboard triangular template, base 7 inches/18 cm and sides 8 inches/20 cm, to cut out the croissants.

Brush the triangles lightly with the egg glaze. Roll into croissant shapes, starting at the base and tucking the point underneath to prevent unrolling while cooking. Brush again with the glaze. Place on an ungreased baking sheet and let double in size. Bake for 15–20 minutes until golden brown.

CROQUE MONSIEUR

INGREDIENTS

1 tbsp butter

4 slices bread

4 thin slices good-quality ham

4 tbsp grated mozzarella cheese

2 tbsp plain yogurt

salt and pepper

1 tbsp chopped fresh parsley

SERVES 2

Butter the bread slices and lay them on top of each other, buttered-sides together. Place the ham on top of the sandwiches and sprinkle a little of the grated cheese over the top without pressing them together.

Heat a nonstick skillet large enough to take 2 sandwiches. Place the top slices of bread (with the ham and cheese on top), buttered-side down, into the skillet. Top with the remaining slices of bread, buttered-side up. Cook until the base of each sandwich is golden brown.

Preheat the broiler to hot. Mix the remaining cheese, yogurt, and salt and pepper to taste together. Remove the skillet from the heat and spread an equal quantity of the yogurt mixture on top of each sandwich. Place under the preheated broiler and cook until lightly browned. Sprinkle with the chopped parsley and serve.

Vary this recipe by experimenting with different kinds of bread, such as rye or sourdough. Although ham is the traditional filling for this classic French sandwich, slices of turkey or roast chicken make delicious alternatives.

SAUSAGES WITH MUSHROOMS, BACON, TOMATOES & FRIED BREAD

Prepare the sausages up to 24 hours in advance and refrigerate them until required. Bake for 15 minutes before serving. Add fried, poached, or scrambled eggs for a real brunch feast!

INGREDIENTS

4 good-quality herbed sausages

4 tbsp grated Cheddar cheese

4 unsmoked lean bacon slices

2 tomatoes, halved horizontally

salt and pepper

1 tbsp butter

1 tbsp olive oil

4½ oz/125 g white mushrooms, sliced

4 slices bread, crusts removed and buttered on both sides

2 tbsp chopped fresh parsley

SERVES 2

Preheat the oven to 350°F/180°C. Prick the sausages lightly, place in a roasting pan and roast for 10 minutes. Remove and let cool. Make a slit in the sausages with a sharp knife and stuff each sausage with 1 tablespoon of the grated cheese. Wrap a bacon slice around each sausage, tucking in the ends to secure. Return to the oven for an additional 20 minutes, or until the bacon is cooked and the sausages are golden brown.

Meanwhile, place the tomatoes, cut-side up, on a baking sheet and season to taste with salt and pepper. Roast for 15–20 minutes. Melt the butter with the oil in a medium skillet over low heat, then add the mushrooms, stirring well to coat. Cover and cook for 5 minutes, or until the mushrooms are soft. Keep warm.

Heat a nonstick skillet over medium heat and cook the buttered bread in batches until golden brown on both sides. Keep warm.

To serve, divide the cooked bread between 2 plates and top with the mushrooms. Add the sausages and tomatoes and sprinkle with parsley.

SCRAMBLED EGGS WITH SMOKED SALMON

INGREDIENTS

8 eggs

⅓ cup light cream

2 tbsp chopped fresh dill, plus extra for garnishing

salt and pepper

3½ oz/100 g smoked salmon, cut into small pieces

2 tbsp butter

slices rustic bread, toasted

SERVES 4

Break the eggs into a large bowl and whisk together with the cream and dill. Season to taste with pepper and a little salt – the smoked salmon may be salty, so do not add too much salt. Add the smoked salmon and mix to combine.

Melt the butter in a large nonstick skillet and pour in the egg and smoked salmon mixture. Using a wooden spatula, gently scrape the egg away from the sides of the skillet as it starts to set and swirl the skillet slightly to allow the uncooked egg to fill the surface.

When the eggs are almost cooked but still creamy, remove from the heat and spoon onto the prepared toast. Serve at once, garnished with a sprig of dill.

As a variation, try substituting smoked trout and snipped chives or even fresh crabmeat—delicious!

MUSHROOM BRUSCHETTA

These bruschetta can be served as an accompaniment to drinks, as a starter or as a snack at any time, but are particularly suitable for brunch.

INGREDIENTS

12 slices baguette, each 1 cm/½ inch thick, or 2 individual baguettes, cut lengthwise

3 tbsp olive oil

2 garlic cloves, crushed

8 oz/225 g crimini mushrooms, sliced

8 oz/225 g mixed wild mushrooms

2 tsp lemon juice

salt and pepper

2 tbsp chopped fresh parsley

SERVES 4

Preheat the broiler to medium. Toast the bread under the hot broiler until golden on both sides. Keep warm.

Meanwhile, heat the oil in a skillet. Add the garlic and cook gently for a few seconds, then add the crimini mushrooms. Cook, stirring constantly, over a high heat for 3 minutes.

Add the wild mushrooms and cook for an additional 2 minutes. Stir in the lemon juice. Season to taste with salt and pepper and stir in the chopped parsley. Spoon the mushroom mixture on to the hot toast and serve.

SEARED SALMON WITH QUICK HOLLANDAISE SAUCE & BABY SPINACH

INGREDIENTS

1 tbsp each dried thyme, dried rosemary, dried oregano, and mild paprika

1 tsp garlic powder

2 tsp cumin seeds

1 tbsp sea salt

4 portions salmon fillet, skin removed

1 tbsp vegetable oil

scant 3½ cups baby spinach

QUICK HOLLANDAISE SAUCE

3 egg yolks

1¾ sticks butter

1 tbsp lemon juice

pepper

SERVES 4

Combine the dried herbs, paprika, garlic powder, cumin seeds, and sea salt in a small grinder and process until smooth. Alternatively, grind by hand using a mortar and pestle. Rub 1 tablespoon of the mixture into the top of each of the salmon fillets.

Heat the oil in a large skillet and cook the salmon, spice-side down, for 2–3 minutes, or until golden brown. Turn over and continue cooking until the salmon is cooked to your liking. Do not overcook or the salmon will be dry.

To make the hollandaise sauce, place the egg yolks in a blender or food processor. Melt the butter in a small pan until bubbling. With the motor running, gradually add the hot butter in a steady stream until the sauce is thick and creamy. Add the lemon juice, and a little warm water if the sauce is too thick, then season to taste with pepper. Remove from the blender or food processor and keep warm.

Divide the baby spinach equally among four plates, place the cooked salmon on top, and spoon over the sauce. Serve at once.

This recipe makes more spice mixture than you will need but it is difficult to make less. Store the leftover mixture in an airtight container for up to two months. Try it on broiled chicken or steak for a quick lunch or dinner dish.

SAUSAGE & POTATO FRITTATA

INGREDIENTS

4 pork sausages or vegetarian sausages

corn oil, for cooking

4 boiled potatoes, cooled and diced

8 cherry tomatoes

4 eggs, beaten

salt and pepper

SERVES 3–4

Preheat the broiler to medium-high. Arrange the sausages on a foil-lined broiler pan and cook under the preheated broiler, turning occasionally, for 12–15 minutes, or until cooked through and golden brown. Let cool slightly, then slice into bite-size pieces.

Meanwhile, heat a little oil in a medium-size (10-inch/25-cm), heavy-bottom skillet with a heatproof handle over medium heat. Add the potatoes and cook until golden brown and crisp all over, then add the tomatoes and cook for an additional 2 minutes. Arrange the sausages in the skillet so that there is an even distribution of potatoes, tomatoes, and sausages.

Add a little more oil to the skillet if it seems dry. Season the beaten eggs to taste and pour the mixture over the ingredients in the skillet. Cook for 3 minutes, without stirring or disturbing the eggs. Place the skillet under the preheated broiler for 3 minutes, or until the top is just cooked. Cut into wedges to serve.

BACON & TOMATO SCRAMBLE

INGREDIENTS

8 lean Canadian bacon slices

2 beefsteak or 4 regular tomatoes, halved

4 eggs

3 tbsp milk

salt and pepper

1 tbsp snipped fresh chives, plus extra to garnish (optional)

1 tbsp sweet butter

SERVES 4

Preheat the broiler to high and cover the broiler rack with foil. Arrange the bacon on the foil and cook under the preheated broiler for 3–4 minutes on each side, or until crisp. About 3 minutes before the end of cooking time, add the tomatoes, cut-side up, and cook for the remainder of the cooking time.

Meanwhile, beat the eggs, milk, and salt and pepper to taste in a medium-size bowl, then stir in the chives.

Melt the butter in a nonstick skillet over medium heat, pour in the egg mixture, and cook, stirring gently with a wooden spoon, for 5–6 minutes, or until lightly set.

Arrange the egg scramble with the cooked bacon and tomatoes on warmed serving plates and serve at once. Sprinkle with extra snipped chives, if desired.

POTATO CAKES WITH BACON & MAPLE SYRUP

Making potato cakes according to this method is an ideal way to use up leftover mashed potatoes.

INGREDIENTS

4 oz/115 g cold mashed potatoes

scant 1 cup milk

½ cup self-rising flour

pinch of salt

1 egg, beaten

corn oil, for cooking

8 good-quality bacon slices, broiled until crisp

1½ tbsp maple syrup

SERVES 4

Put the mashed potatoes and milk into a food processor or blender and process to a thin purée.

Sift the flour and salt into a mixing bowl, make a well in the center of the flour, and add the beaten egg and potato purée. Using a balloon whisk, gradually mix the flour into the liquid ingredients, whisking well to make a smooth, creamy, fairly thick batter.

Heat a little oil in a large, nonstick skillet. Pour a small ladleful of batter per cake into the skillet—you will probably fit about three in the skillet at one time. Cook for 2 minutes on each side until golden brown. Remove from the skillet and keep warm while you cook the remaining potato cakes.

Divide the cakes among four warmed plates, top each serving with 2 bacon slices, and drizzle with maple syrup.

BACON BUNS

INGREDIENTS

8 smoked Canadian bacon slices

6 tomatoes

1⅛ cups plain cottage cheese

freshly ground black pepper

4 large seeded whole-wheat or white bread rolls

2 scallions, chopped

SERVES 4

Preheat the broiler to high. Remove any visible fat and rind from the bacon and cut 4 of the tomatoes in half. Place the bacon and tomatoes, cut-side up, under the preheated broiler and cook, turning the bacon over halfway through, for 8–10 minutes, or until the bacon is crisp and the tomatoes are softened. Remove the tomatoes and bacon from the broiler and drain the bacon on paper towels to help remove any excess fat. Keep the bacon and tomatoes warm.

Meanwhile, cut the remaining tomatoes into bite-size pieces and combine with the cottage cheese in a bowl. Cut the bacon into bite-size pieces and stir into the cottage cheese mixture. Season to taste with pepper.

Cut the bread rolls in half and divide the bacon filling evenly over each roll base. Sprinkle the scallions over the filling and cover with the roll tops. Serve at once with the broiled tomatoes.

Although bacon is the suggestion for this recipe, chopped roast chicken or even fresh crabmeat would make delicious alternatives.

STUFFED PORTOBELLO MUSHROOMS WITH SHAVED PARMESAN

Mushrooms absorb water, so never soak them to clean them. The best way to clean them is simply to wipe them over with a damp cloth. For Parmesan shavings, run a vegetable peeler down the side of the cheese.

INGREDIENTS

12 large portobello mushrooms, wiped over and stems removed

2 tbsp corn oil, plus extra for oiling

1 fennel bulb, stalks removed, finely chopped

scant ½ cup sun-dried tomatoes, finely chopped

2 garlic cloves, crushed

generous 1 cup grated fontina cheese

scant ½ cup freshly grated Parmesan cheese

3 tbsp chopped fresh basil

salt and pepper

1 tbsp olive oil

fresh Parmesan cheese shavings

1 tbsp chopped fresh parsley, to serve

SERVES 4

Preheat the oven to 350°F/180°C. Lightly oil a large ovenproof dish. Place 8 of the mushrooms, cup-side up, in the dish and chop the remaining 4 mushrooms finely.

Heat the corn oil in a nonstick skillet, add the chopped mushrooms, fennel, sun-dried tomatoes, and garlic and cook over low heat until the vegetables are soft but not browned. Remove from the heat and let cool.

When cool, add the cheeses, basil, and salt and pepper to taste. Mix well. Brush the mushrooms lightly with the olive oil and fill each cavity with a spoonful of the vegetable filling. Bake for 20–25 minutes, or until the mushrooms are tender and the filling is heated through.

Top with Parmesan shavings and parsley and serve at once, allowing 2 mushrooms for each person.

BRUNCH BRUSCHETTA

INGREDIENTS

1 large ripe tomato, diced

2 scallions, finely sliced

1 small fresh buffalo mozzarella cheese, diced

½ ripe avocado, diced

1½ tsp balsamic vinegar

2 tbsp extra virgin olive oil

salt and pepper

4 slices ciabatta bread, toasted, to serve

2 tbsp shredded fresh basil leaves,
to garnish

SERVES 2

Mix the tomato, scallions, cheese, avocado, balsamic vinegar, and half of the oil together in a medium bowl. Season to taste with salt and pepper.

Drizzle the remaining oil over the ciabatta toast and top with the tomato mixture. Garnish with basil and serve at once.

Prepare the topping ingredients up to one hour in advance, adding the avocado and balsamic vinegar just before serving. Buffalo mozzarella is available at some Italian delicatessens and large supermarkets.

CHEESE & HERB SOUFFLÉS WITH SAUTÉED MUSHROOMS

Do not be tempted to overfill the soufflé dishes, since the mixture may rise and fall over the sides. For best results, use only very fresh eggs. The cooked soufflés without the topping will keep for up to 24 hours in the refrigerator.

INGREDIENTS

½ stick butter, plus extra, melted, for greasing

⅓ cup all-purpose flour

⅔ cup milk

generous 1 cup ricotta cheese

4 egg yolks

2 tbsp finely chopped fresh parsley

2 tbsp finely chopped fresh thyme

1 tbsp finely chopped fresh rosemary

salt and pepper

6 egg whites

scant 1 cup light cream

6 tbsp grated Parmesan cheese

sautéed white mushrooms, to serve

MAKES 6 SOUFFLÉS

Preheat the oven to 350°F/180°C. Brush six 3½-inch/9-cm soufflé dishes well with melted butter and set aside. Melt the butter in a medium pan, add the flour, and cook for 30 seconds, stirring constantly. Whisk in the milk and continue whisking over low heat until the mixture thickens. Cook for an additional 30 seconds. Remove from the heat and beat in the ricotta. Add the egg yolks and herbs and season well with salt and pepper.

Beat the egg whites in a clean bowl until they form stiff peaks and gently fold them through the ricotta mixture. Spoon into the prepared dishes, filling them just to the top. Place in a baking dish and pour in enough boiling water to come halfway up the sides of the dishes. Bake for 15–20 minutes, or until the soufflés are well risen and browned. Remove from the oven, let cool for 10 minutes, then gently ease out of their molds. Place in a lightly greased ovenproof dish and cover with plastic wrap.

Increase the oven temperature to 400°F/200°C. Remove the plastic wrap and pour the cream evenly over the soufflés, sprinkle with Parmesan, and return to the oven for an additional 15 minutes. Serve at once with sautéed mushrooms.

SWEET POTATO, MINT & FETA RÖSTI

INGREDIENTS

1 lb 5 oz/600 g sweet potatoes, peeled and grated

1 egg, lightly beaten

⅓ cup all-purpose flour

5 tbsp butter, melted

3½ oz/100 g feta cheese, crumbled

3 tbsp chopped fresh mint

salt and pepper

1 tbsp vegetable oil

4 tbsp sour cream

2 tbsp chopped fresh herbs, to garnish

SERVES 4

Preheat the oven to 325°F/160°C. Cover a baking sheet with parchment paper. Mix the grated sweet potato with the egg, flour, melted butter, feta, and mint until well combined. Season to taste with salt and pepper.

Heat the oil in a large nonstick skillet over medium heat. Spoon large tablespoons of the mixture into the skillet, shaping them into patties and flattening slightly. Cook on both sides in batches until golden.

Slide the rösti on to the prepared baking sheet and bake for 15 minutes, or until crisp. Place 2 rösti on each plate, top with a tablespoon of sour cream, and garnish with a little chopped herbs. Serve at once.

Use the grater blade on your food processor to make the job of grating the sweet potato really easy. Serve with slices of smoked salmon or crispy bacon for an interesting variation.

VEGETABLE RÖSTI

Quick and easy to prepare and cook, this is ideal to serve both as a main component of breakfast or brunch, or as an accompaniment to a main meal.

INGREDIENTS

1 carrot, grated

1 zucchini, grated

1 sweet potato, grated

8 scallions, finely chopped or shredded

pepper

1 egg white, beaten

2 tsp extra-virgin olive oil

SERVES 4

Mix all the vegetables together and season with pepper to taste, then stir in the egg white. Using clean hands, form into 8 small patties. Press them firmly together.

Heat the oil in a nonstick skillet and cook the patties over gentle heat for 5–6 minutes, or until golden. Turn over halfway through the cooking time and press down with the back of a spatula. Do this in two batches to prevent the skillet from being overcrowded.

As soon as the patties are cooked, serve immediately.

SWEET POTATO BLINIS

INGREDIENTS

4 oz/115 g sweet potatoes, peeled and cut into chunks

pepper

1 tsp ground allspice

generous ⅓ cup whole-wheat flour

1 egg

⅔ cup milk

1 egg white

FILLING

3 oz/85 g prosciutto

3 tomatoes, thickly sliced

⅔ cup cream cheese

1 tbsp finely grated lemon rind

1 tbsp chopped fresh parsley

1 oz/25 g arugula leaves

SERVES 4–6

Cook the sweet potatoes in boiling water over medium heat for 15 minutes, or until soft. Drain and mash until smooth, then season with pepper to taste and stir in the ground allspice and flour. Place in a mixing bowl.

Add the whole egg and beat it into the mashed sweet potatoes, then gradually stir in the milk to give a thick batter consistency. Set aside until required.

Prepare the filling. Preheat the broiler. Cut the prosciutto into strips. Place the tomatoes on a foil-lined broiler rack and, just before serving, cook under the preheated hot broiler for 3–4 minutes, or until hot. Blend the cream cheese with the lemon rind and parsley. Set aside.

Whisk the egg white until stiff and stir it into the sweet potato batter. Heat a nonstick skillet until hot, then place 3–4 spoonfuls of the batter in the skillet and swirl to form a 3-inch/7.5-cm circle. Cook for 2–3 minutes, or until set, then turn over and cook for an additional 2–3 minutes, or until golden. Keep warm while you cook the remaining batter.

Place 2–3 blinis on a plate and top with a little arugula, prosciutto, and broiled tomato, then spoon over a little of the cream cheese and serve.

These blinis are very versatile. Try them for an informal brunch, or as an unusual dinner party appetizer, or make them smaller and serve as canapés.

The Late Brunch

SANDWICHES WITH TOMATO CHILE JELLY

The Tomato Chile Jelly can be made up to three months in advance and stored in the cupboard. Refrigerate once the jelly has been opened. Cheddar cheese makes a nice alternative to fontina.

INGREDIENTS

4 slices fontina cheese

4 slices bread

3 eggs

salt and pepper

2 tbsp butter

arugula leaves, to serve

tomato chile jelly

1 tbsp corn oil

1 onion, diced

1 red bell pepper, seeded and diced

1 tbsp dried chile flakes

2 large tomatoes, chopped

generous 1 cup cider vinegar

generous ½ cup brown sugar

SERVES 2

To make the tomato chile jelly, heat the oil in a medium pan over low heat and cook the diced onion for 5 minutes, or until soft but not brown. Add the diced red bell pepper and chile flakes and cook for an additional 2 minutes, then add the tomatoes, vinegar, and sugar. Bring to a boil, then reduce the heat and let simmer for 45 minutes, stirring occasionally, until the mixture thickens to a jelly consistency.

Divide the cheese between 2 slices of bread. Spread each with a tablespoon of the tomato chile jelly and cover with another slice of bread. Beat the eggs and salt and pepper to taste in a wide dish. Dip one side of each sandwich into the egg mixture and let stand for 1 minute. Repeat with the other side.

Heat the butter in a small nonstick skillet over low heat and add one sandwich at a time. Cook for 2 minutes, or until golden brown and the cheese is starting to melt, then turn and cook for an additional 2 minutes. Repeat with the remaining sandwich.

Serve with a handful of fresh arugula leaves and some more tomato chile jelly on the side.

BAGELS WITH LEEKS & CHEESE

INGREDIENTS

2 leeks

2 tbsp butter

generous 1 cup grated Gruyère cheese

2 scallions, finely chopped

1 tbsp chopped fresh parsley

salt and pepper

2 fresh bagels

SERVES 2

Trim the leeks, discarding the green ends, and split down the center, leaving the root intact. Wash well to remove any grit and slice finely, discarding the root.

Melt the butter over low heat in a large skillet and add the leeks. Cook, stirring constantly, for 5 minutes, or until the leeks are soft and slightly browned. Let cool.

Preheat the broiler. Mix the cooled leeks, grated cheese, scallions, parsley, and salt and pepper to taste together. Split the bagels and toast lightly on the bottom. Spread the cheese mixture over the top of each bagel and place under the preheated broiler until bubbling and golden brown. Serve at once.

This leek and Gruyère cheese mixture is a perfect topping for bagels, but also tastes delicious served on slices of sourdough toast, for a change.

TUSCAN BEANS ON CIABATTA TOAST WITH FRESH HERBS

This recipe also works well with cannellini beans. This dish can be made in advance and reheated as required.

INGREDIENTS

1 tbsp olive oil

1 small onion, finely diced

1 garlic clove, crushed

9 oz/250 g canned lima beans, drained and rinsed

⅓ cup water

1 tbsp tomato paste

1 tsp balsamic vinegar

1 tbsp chopped fresh parsley

1 tbsp torn fresh basil

salt and pepper

slices ciabatta bread, toasted, to serve

SERVES 2

Heat the oil in a medium skillet and cook the onion over low heat until soft. Add the garlic and cook for an additional 1 minute, then add the lima beans, water, and tomato paste. Bring to a boil, stirring occasionally, and cook for 2 minutes.

Add the balsamic vinegar, parsley, and basil and stir to combine. Season to taste with salt and pepper and serve over slices of toasted ciabatta.

TOMATO BREAD

INGREDIENTS

6–8 slices French bread or other crusty bread

3–4 tomatoes, halved

1–2 garlic cloves (optional)

olive oil, for drizzling (optional)

SERVES 4

To serve this at its simplest, rub the slices of bread with the tomato halves, letting the juice and seeds soak into the bread. If the bread is soft, you can toast it first.

Other options are to flavor it with garlic in the same way, or drizzle olive oil over the top of the tomato.

If you like, you can garnish the tomato bread with thin strips of drained, canned anchovies

SCRAMBLED EGGS WITH ASPARAGUS

INGREDIENTS

½ stick butter

4 oz/115 g baby asparagus spears, diagonally sliced

3 oz/85 g button mushrooms, sliced

4 eggs

3 tbsp light cream

salt and pepper

4 thick slices cooked ham

1–2 tbsp snipped fresh chives

SERVES 4

Melt half the butter in a skillet over medium heat, add the asparagus and mushrooms, and cook, stirring frequently, for 5 minutes, or until softened. Remove from the skillet, drain if necessary, and keep warm.

Beat the eggs with the cream, and salt and pepper to taste in a medium-size bowl.

Melt the remaining butter in a nonstick pan over medium heat. Pour in the egg mixture and cook, stirring gently with a wooden spoon, for 5–6 minutes, or until lightly set.

Arrange the ham on serving plates, top with the asparagus and mushrooms, then the egg scramble. Sprinkle with the chives and serve at once.

CHIVE SCRAMBLED EGGS WITH BRIOCHE

INGREDIENTS

4 eggs

generous ⅓ cup light cream

salt and pepper

2 tbsp snipped fresh chives, plus
4 whole fresh chives to garnish

2 tbsp butter

4 slices brioche loaf, lightly toasted

SERVES 2

Break the eggs into a medium bowl and whisk gently with the cream. Season to taste with salt and pepper, and add the snipped chives.

Melt the butter in a skillet and pour in the egg mixture. Let set slightly, then move the mixture toward the center of the pan using a wooden spoon as the eggs start to cook. Continue in this way until the eggs are cooked but still creamy.

Place the toasted brioche slices in the centers of 2 plates and spoon over the scrambled eggs. Serve at once, garnished with whole chives.

Resist the temptation to cook the eggs completely. The best scrambled eggs should still look just a little undercooked—they will carry on cooking in their own heat once you have served them.

MEXICAN EGGS

Be careful when handling chiles, don't touch your eyes or lips, and always wash your hands thoroughly afterward.

INGREDIENTS

8 large eggs

2 tbsp milk

pepper

1 tsp olive oil

1 red bell pepper, seeded and thinly sliced

½ fresh red chile, finely diced

1 fresh chorizo sausage, skinned and sliced

4 tbsp chopped fresh cilantro

4 slices toasted whole-wheat bread, to serve

SERVES 4

Beat the eggs, milk, and pepper to taste in a large bowl. Set aside.

Heat the oil in a nonstick skillet over medium heat, add the red bell pepper and chile and cook, stirring frequently, for 5 minutes, or until the red bell pepper is soft and browned in places. Add the chorizo and cook until just browned. Transfer to a warmed plate and set aside.

Return the skillet to the heat, add the egg mixture, and cook to a soft scramble. Add the chorizo mixture, stir to combine and sprinkle over the cilantro. Serve at once on toasted whole-wheat bread.

FRITTATA WITH SPICES

INGREDIENTS

2 tbsp vegetable oil

1 small red onion, diced

1 tbsp fennel seeds

1 tsp dried chile flakes

9 oz/250 g canned chickpeas, drained and rinsed

1 cup frozen peas, thawed

1 tomato, diced

8 eggs

3 tbsp chopped fresh cilantro

salt and pepper

TO SERVE

4 tbsp tomato chutney

4 tbsp plain yogurt

SERVES 4

Preheat the broiler to hot. Heat the oil in a 12-inch/30-cm nonstick skillet over low heat and cook the onion for a few minutes, or until soft but not brown. Add the fennel seeds and chile flakes and cook for an additional 1 minute, then stir in the chickpeas, peas, and diced tomato.

Break the eggs into a bowl and beat lightly with a fork. Mix in the cilantro and season to taste with salt and pepper. Pour the egg mixture over the ingredients in the skillet and cook until just starting to set. Place under the broiler until the egg has fully set and the frittata is lightly brown. Serve, cut into wedges, with tomato chutney and yogurt on the side.

This frittata is delicious served hot or warm. It can be made a few hours in advance and reheated in a warm oven just before serving.

WILD MUSHROOM OMELET

If fresh wild mushrooms are unavailable, look for dried porcini mushrooms (cèpes). Cover with warm water and soak for 20 minutes, then drain and use.

INGREDIENTS

1 tsp extra-virgin olive oil

1 small onion, cut into wedges

2–3 garlic cloves, crushed

3 oz/85 g assorted wild mushrooms, cleaned and cut in half if large

3 oz/85 g closed cup mushrooms, wiped and sliced

1 zucchini, trimmed and grated

2 eggs, plus 2 egg whites

salt and pepper

1 yellow bell pepper, seeded, peeled, and cut into strips

1 tbsp freshly grated Parmesan cheese (optional)

1 tbsp shredded fresh basil

TO SERVE

tossed green salad

warm whole-wheat bread (optional)

SERVES 2–4

Heat the oil in a large nonstick skillet and cook the onion and garlic over very gentle heat for 3 minutes. Cover the skillet during cooking. Stir occasionally. Add the mushrooms and cook for an additional 4–5 minutes, or until the mushrooms have softened slightly. Add the grated zucchini.

Beat the whole eggs with the egg whites, salt and pepper to taste, and 2 tablespoons of water. Pour into the skillet and increase the heat slightly, then cook, drawing the egg into the center of the skillet from the edges with a fork or spatula.

When the omelet is set on the bottom, sprinkle the strips of yellow bell pepper over it, followed by the Parmesan cheese, if using, and the basil. Cook for an additional 3–4 minutes, or until set to personal preference.

Serve the omelet cut into wedges with a tossed green salad, and, if you like, warm chunks of whole-wheat bread.

ZUCCHINI FRITTERS WITH EGGS & CARAMELIZED ONIONS

INGREDIENTS

2 tbsp extra-virgin olive oil

5 red onions, sliced

1 tbsp brown sugar

salt and pepper

scant 1½ cups self-rising flour

1 egg, lightly beaten, plus 4 eggs
for poaching or frying

scant 1 cup milk

2 zucchini, grated

1 cup corn oil

SERVES 4

Heat the olive oil in a large heavy-bottom pan over medium heat, add the onions, and cook for 5 minutes, or until softened. Stir in the sugar and reduce the heat, cover, and cook for 30 minutes, or until the onions are deep brown in color, stirring occasionally. Season to taste with salt and pepper and let cool.

To make the fritters, place the flour in a large bowl and make a well in the center. Whisk the beaten egg and milk together and incorporate into the flour, using a wooden spoon to make a batter. Season to taste with salt and pepper and stir in the grated zucchini.

Heat the corn oil in a wide deep-sided pan and drop in tablespoons of the batter. Cook until golden brown on both sides, turning once. Drain on paper towels and keep warm.

Poach or fry the eggs, as you prefer. To serve, place 2 fritters on each individual plate, place an egg on top, and spoon over some of the caramelized onions. Serve at once.

Make the caramelized onions in advance and store in the refrigerator for up to a week. If the batter for the fritters seems too thick, stir in a little extra milk.

MUSHROOM BRIOCHES

These mushroom-filled brioches can also be served as a starter or a light lunch.

INGREDIENTS

6 small brioches

5 tbsp olive oil

1 garlic clove, crushed

2 shallots, finely chopped

12 oz/350 g crimini mushrooms, sliced

1 tsp Dijon mustard

2 tbsp dry sherry

1 tsp chopped fresh thyme

⅔ cup heavy cream

salt and pepper

herb sprigs, to garnish

SERVES 6

Preheat the oven to 200°C/400°F. Cut the tops off the brioches and scoop out the insides of each one to make a hollow case. Brush the insides of the brioches with 3 tablespoons of the oil. Place them on a baking tray and cook in the oven for 10–12 minutes, until crisp.

Meanwhile, heat the remaining oil in a saucepan. Add the garlic and shallots, and cook for 3 minutes, until soft. Add the mushrooms and cook gently for 5 minutes, stirring occasionally.

Stir in the mustard, sherry, thyme, cream, and salt and pepper to taste, then cook for a few minutes until the mixture is slightly reduced and thickened. Spoon into the brioche cases and serve immediately garnished with herb sprigs.

ASPARAGUS WITH POACHED EGGS & PARMESAN

INGREDIENTS

10½ oz/300 g asparagus, trimmed

4 large eggs

3 oz/85 g Parmesan cheese

pepper

SERVES 4

Bring 2 pans of water to a boil. Add the asparagus to 1 pan, return to a simmer, and cook for 5 minutes, or until just tender.

Meanwhile, reduce the heat of the second pan to a simmer and carefully crack in the eggs, one at a time. Poach for 3 minutes, or until the whites are just set but the yolks are still soft. Remove with a slotted spoon.

Drain the asparagus and divide among 4 warmed plates. Top each plate of asparagus with an egg and shave over the cheese. Season to taste with pepper and serve at once.

Poach the eggs for a little longer than the suggested three minutes if you prefer your yolks a little firmer.

SMOKED SALMON, FETA & DILL PHYLLO PACKAGES

Phyllo dough dries out very quickly, so be sure to keep unused portions covered with a damp cloth as you work.

INGREDIENTS

5½ oz/150 g feta cheese, crumbled

generous 1 cup ricotta cheese

5½ oz/150 g smoked salmon, diced

2 tbsp chopped fresh dill

2 tbsp snipped fresh chives

salt and pepper

12 sheets phyllo dough

7 tbsp butter, melted, plus extra for greasing

4 tbsp dried bread crumbs

6 tsp fennel seeds

MAKES 6 PACKAGES

Preheat the oven to 350°F/180°C. Lightly grease a baking sheet. In a large bowl, combine the feta, ricotta, smoked salmon, dill, and chives. Season to taste with salt and pepper.

Lay out a sheet of pastry on your counter and brush well with melted butter. Sprinkle over 2 teaspoons of the bread crumbs and cover with a second sheet of pastry. Brush with butter and spread a large tablespoon of the salmon mixture on one end of the pastry. Roll the pastry up, folding in the sides, to enclose the salmon completely and create a neat package. Place on the prepared baking sheet, brush the top of the package with butter and sprinkle over 1 teaspoon of the fennel seeds. Repeat with the remaining ingredients to make 6 packages.

Bake the packages for 25–30 minutes, or until the pastry is golden brown. Serve the packages warm.

SMOKED SALMON, RED ONION & GOAT CHEESE TARTS

INGREDIENTS

9 oz/250 g good-quality puff pastry

all-purpose flour, for rolling

1 egg, lightly beaten with 1 tbsp milk

1 small red onion, sliced

3½ oz/100 g goat cheese, crumbled

4 slices smoked salmon

pepper

SERVES 4

Preheat the oven to 400°F/200°C. Roll the puff pastry out to ¼ inch/5 mm thick on a lightly floured counter and cut into 4 even-size squares. Place on an ungreased baking sheet and brush each square lightly with the egg mixture. Divide the sliced onion evenly among the tarts and top with goat cheese.

Bake for 20–25 minutes, or until the pastry has risen and is golden brown. Let cool slightly, then top with the slices of smoked salmon and season to taste with pepper. Serve at once.

Look for puff pastry made with butter for the very best results. There are many different types of goat cheese available—a mild, creamy variety is perfect for this recipe. Substitute Camembert or Brie, cut into pieces, if you prefer.

SPANISH TORTILLA WITH ROASTED BELL PEPPERS & SPICY CHORIZO

Manchego cheese is a firm Spanish cheese made from sheep's milk. Substitute a good-quality Parmesan or Romano if you have trouble finding it. Don't add oil when cooking the chorizo sausage as it already contains a high percentage of fat.

INGREDIENTS

2 red bell peppers, halved and seeded

2 small chorizo sausages, diced

1 tbsp olive oil

2 potatoes, peeled and diced

handful of fresh basil leaves, torn into pieces

6 large eggs, lightly beaten

6 tbsp grated Manchego cheese

salt and pepper

SERVES 6

Preheat the oven to 400°F/200°C. Place the red bell peppers on a lined baking sheet and roast for 15 minutes, or until the skins are black. Remove from the oven and cover with a dish towel until cool. When cool, peel away the skins and dice the flesh.

Meanwhile, cook the diced chorizo in a 12-inch/30-cm nonstick skillet until it is brown and the fat is rendered. Drain on paper towels. Wipe out the skillet, then heat the oil and cook the diced potatoes for 5 minutes, or until soft and lightly browned. Return the chorizo to the skillet with the potatoes and add the diced red bell peppers and torn basil leaves.

Mix the eggs and grated cheese together and season to taste with salt and pepper. Pour over the ingredients in the skillet, using a wooden spoon to distribute the ingredients evenly. Let cook for a few minutes over low heat until the egg has started to set. To finish the tortilla, place the skillet under a preheated hot broiler to brown lightly. Slide onto a serving plate and cut into wedges to serve.

FOCACCIA WITH ROASTED CHERRY TOMATOES, BASIL & CRISPY PANCETTA

INGREDIENTS

1 lb 2 oz/500 g white bread flour, plus extra for kneading and rolling

1 tbsp dried basil

½ tsp sugar

2 tsp rapid-rise dried yeast

2 tsp salt

generous 1¼ cups water, lukewarm

2 tbsp olive oil, plus extra for oiling

TOPPING

14 oz/400 g cherry tomatoes

1 tbsp olive oil, plus extra for oiling and drizzling

salt and pepper

7 oz/200 g thick pancetta, diced

4 tbsp chopped fresh basil

SERVES 4–6

Place the flour, dried basil, sugar, yeast, and salt in a bowl. Combine the water and oil and mix with the dry ingredients to form a soft dough, adding more water if the dough appears too dry. Turn out onto a lightly floured counter and knead for 10 minutes, or until the dough bounces back when pressed lightly with your finger. Place the dough in a lightly oiled bowl and cover with plastic wrap. Leave in a warm place for 1 hour, or until doubled in size.

Meanwhile, preheat the oven to 275°F/140°C. Place the tomatoes on a baking sheet covered with parchment paper, sprinkle with oil, and season to taste with salt and pepper. Bake for 30 minutes, or until the tomatoes are soft.

Increase the oven temperature to 425°F/220°C. Remove the dough from the bowl and knead again briefly. Shape into a rectangle and place on a lightly oiled baking sheet, turning the dough over to oil both sides. Make rough indentations in the dough using your fingers. Top with the tomatoes and pancetta. Sprinkle with salt and pepper. Leave in a warm place for 10 minutes for the dough to rise again. Bake for 15–20 minutes, or until golden brown and cooked through. Drizzle with oil and top with fresh basil. Serve warm.

Be sure to roll the final bread dough out fairly thinly as it rises quite a bit in the final stage. Take care not to bake the tomatoes for too long, otherwise they will lose their shape.

SMOKED SALMON WITH BROCCOLI

INGREDIENTS

8 oz/225 g broccoli

4 eggs

2 tsp lemon juice (optional)

8 oz/225 g smoked salmon

whole-wheat bread, to serve

DRESSING

⅔ cup cream cheese

1–1½ tsp Dijon mustard

2 tsp snipped fresh chives

SERVES 4

Divide the broccoli into spears, then cook in boiling water for 5–6 minutes, or until tender. Drain and keep warm while you poach the eggs.

To poach the eggs, half-fill a large skillet with water, then add the lemon juice, if using, and bring to a boil. Reduce the heat to a simmer, then carefully break 1 egg into a cup and slip into the simmering water. Repeat with the remaining eggs. Poach the eggs for 3–4 minutes, or until set to personal preference.

Meanwhile, divide the smoked salmon among four individual plates. Stir all the dressing ingredients together in a mixing cup until blended.

Place the broccoli spears on the plates and top each with a poached egg, then spoon over a little dressing and serve. Serve with whole-wheat bread.

PROSCIUTTO WITH MELON & ASPARAGUS

INGREDIENTS

8 oz/225 g baby asparagus spears

1 small or ½ medium-size canteloupe melon

2 oz/55 g prosciutto, thinly sliced

5½ oz/150 g mixed salad greens

heaping ½ cup fresh raspberries

1 tbsp freshly shaved Parmesan cheese

1 tbsp balsamic vinegar

2 tbsp raspberry vinegar

2 tbsp orange juice

SERVES 4

Trim the asparagus, cutting in half if very long. Cook in lightly boiling water over medium heat for 5 minutes, or until tender. Drain and plunge into cold water, then drain again and set aside.

Cut the melon in half and scoop out the seeds. Cut into small wedges and cut away the rind. Separate the prosciutto and cut the slices in half, then wrap around the melon wedges.

Arrange the salad greens on a large serving platter and place the melon wedges on top together with the asparagus spears.

Scatter over the raspberries and Parmesan shavings. Place the vinegars and juice in a screw-top jar and shake until blended. Pour over the salad and serve.

When eating melons, it is important that they are ripe, but not over- or underripe. When choosing a melon, a good indication is to gently press one end—it should yield slightly—and to smell it. Ripe melons will give off a sweet, pleasant aroma. Keep out of the refrigerator for best results.

MINI BACON & EGG PASTRIES WITH CHEDDAR

Take care not to force the dough circles into the muffin pans by stretching them as this will lead to the dough shrinking while it is in the oven. Gently ease the dough into the pan so that it fits into the edges before filling the pastries.

INGREDIENTS
butter, for greasing

1 lb 2 oz/500 g prepared plain pie dough

all-purpose flour, for rolling

2 tbsp whole-grain mustard

12 lean rindless bacon slices, diced, cooked, and drained well

12 small eggs

pepper

generous 1 cup grated Cheddar cheese

2 tbsp chopped fresh parsley

MAKES 12 PASTRIES
Preheat the oven to 350°F/180°C. Lightly grease a deep 12-cup muffin pan.

Roll the dough out to a ¼-inch/5-mm thickness on a lightly floured counter and cut out 12 circles approximately 5 inches/13 cm in diameter. Use to line the cups of the muffin pan, gently pleating the sides of the dough as you ease it into the molds. Place ½ teaspoon of the mustard into the base of each pastry shell and top with a little of the bacon.

Break an egg into a cup, spoon the yolk into the pastry shell, then add enough of the white to fill the pastry shell about two-thirds full. Do not overfill. Season to taste with pepper and sprinkle the grated cheese evenly over the tops of the pastries. Bake for 20–25 minutes, or until the egg is set and the cheese is golden brown. Serve warm, sprinkled with chopped parsley.

The Perfect Drinks

SUMMER & CITRUS FRUIT PUNCH

To give this punch a fragrant twist, substitute dry ginger ale for the sparkling water. For an alcoholic version, replace the sparkling water with sparkling white wine.

INGREDIENTS

4 tbsp orange juice

1 tbsp lime juice

scant ½ cup sparkling water

4 ice cubes

12 oz/350 g frozen summer berries, such as blueberries, raspberries, blackberries, and strawberries

whole fresh strawberries, raspberries, black currants, and blackberries on toothpicks, to decorate

SERVES 2

Pour the orange juice, lime juice, and sparkling water into a blender or food processor and process gently until combined.

Put the ice cubes between 2 clean cloths and crush with a rolling pin. Add to the blender with the frozen berries and process until a slushy consistency has been reached.

Pour the mixture into glasses, then decorate with whole strawberries, raspberries, black currants, and blackberries on toothpicks and serve.

BERRY SMOOTHIE

INGREDIENTS
2 tbsp blueberries

6 tbsp raspberries, thawed if frozen

1 tsp honey

scant 1 cup plain yogurt

about 1 heaping tbsp crushed ice

1 tbsp sesame seeds

SERVES 1
Put the blueberries into a food processor or blender and process for
1 minute.

Add the raspberries, honey, and yogurt and process for an additional minute.

Add the ice and sesame seeds and process again for an additional minute.
Pour into a tall glass and serve at once.

For extra flavor, use a honey with a light, delicate aroma,
such as orange blossom or lemon blossom.

ALMOND & BANANA SMOOTHIE

The ripeness of the banana will give this smoothie a naturally sweet taste.

INGREDIENTS

scant 1 cup whole blanched almonds

2½ cups milk

2 ripe bananas, halved

1 tsp vanilla extract

ground cinnamon, for sprinkling

SERVES 3–4

Put the almonds into a food processor and process until very finely chopped. Add the milk, bananas, and vanilla extract, and blend until smooth and creamy.

Pour into glasses and sprinkle with cinnamon.

RISE & SHINE JUICE

INGREDIENTS

4 tomatoes, quartered

scant ½ cup grated carrot

1 tbsp lime juice

SERVES 1

Put the tomatoes, carrot, and lime juice into a blender and process for a few seconds until smooth.

Place a nylon strainer over a bowl and pour in the tomato mixture. Using a spoon, gently push as much of the liquid through the strainer as possible. Discard any pits and pulp remaining in the strainer.

Pour the juice into a glass and serve at once.

It is important to use a nylon strainer rather than one with a metal mesh that might taint the flavor of the juice.

RED BELL PEPPER BOOSTER

This is extremely easy to make and bursting with vitamins. The perfect way to kick-start your day.

INGREDIENTS

1 cup carrot juice

1 cup tomato juice

2 large red bell peppers, seeded and coarsely chopped

1 tbsp lemon juice

freshly ground black pepper

SERVES 2

Pour the carrot juice and tomato juice into a food processor and process gently until combined.

Add the red bell peppers and lemon juice. Season with plenty of freshly ground black pepper and process until smooth. Pour the mixture into tall glasses, add straws, and serve.

BANANA & STRAWBERRY SMOOTHIE

INGREDIENTS
1 banana, sliced

½ cup fresh strawberries, hulled

generous ⅔ cup plain yogurt

SERVE 1
Put the banana, strawberries, and yogurt into a blender and process for a few seconds until smooth.

Pour into a glass and serve at once.

Wiping strawberries with damp paper towels is better than washing them as they easily become waterlogged.

STRAWBERRY & PEACH SMOOTHIE

You can easily vary this recipe to make different-flavored smoothies. Use raspberries or blueberries in place of the strawberries, or a small peeled, pitted mango instead of the apricots. Or try replacing the bananas with a couple of scoops of vanilla or even chocolate ice cream.

INGREDIENTS

¾ cup milk

8 oz/225 g canned peach slices (drained weight)

2 fresh apricots, chopped

14 oz/400 g fresh strawberries

2 fresh bananas, sliced and frozen

SERVES 2

Pour the milk into a blender or food processor. Add the peach slices and gently process until combined. Add the apricots and gently process again until combined.

Pick over the strawberries and hull, reserving one to decorate. Add the strawberries and frozen banana slices and process until smooth. Pour the mixture into glasses. Slice the reserved strawberry and use to decorate the glasses. Serve immediately.

BLACK CURRANT BRACER

INGREDIENTS

⅔ cup frozen black currants

4 scoops black currant sherbet

scant ½ cup sour cream

2 tbsp black currant cordial,
plus extra for drizzling

1 tbsp water

sugar, to taste

few mint leaves

SERVES 2

Put the black currants, sherbet, sour cream, cordial, and water into a food processor and process until smooth. Taste and sweeten with a little sugar if necessary.

Pour into glasses. Drizzle over some cordial, then decorate with the mint leaves and serve.

For a strictly grown-up version, use crème de cassis instead of the cordial.

SPICED LEMON TEA

An aromatic warm drink, which is perfect at any time of year.

INGREDIENTS

1¾ cups water

4 cloves

1 small stick of cinnamon stick

2 tea bags

3–4 tbsp lemon juice

1–2 tbsp brown sugar

slices of lemon

SERVE 2

Put the water, cloves, and cinnamon into a pan and bring to a boil. Remove from the heat and add the tea bags. Let infuse for 5 minutes, then remove the tea bags.

Stir in lemon juice and sugar to taste. Return the pan to the heat and warm through gently.

Remove the pan from the heat and strain the tea into heatproof glasses. Decorate with slices of lemon and serve.

CITRUS ICED TEA

INGREDIENTS

1 ¼ cups water

2 tea bags

scant ½ cup orange juice

4 tbsp lime juice

1–2 tbsp brown sugar

wedge of lime

granulated sugar

8 ice cubes

slices of orange, lemon, or lime, to decorate

SERVES 2

Pour the water into a pan and bring to a boil. Remove from the heat, then add the tea bags and let infuse for 5 minutes. Remove the tea bags and then let the tea cool to room temperature (about 30 minutes). Transfer to a pitcher, then cover with plastic wrap and chill in the refrigerator for at least 45 minutes.

When the tea has chilled, pour in the orange juice and lime juice. Add sugar to taste.

Take two glasses and rub the rims with a wedge of lime, then dip them in granulated sugar to frost. Put the ice cubes into the glasses and pour over the tea. Decorate the rims with slices of fresh orange, lemon, or lime and serve.

The combination of sweet and sharp citrus flavors turns
this into an irresistible drink.

IRISH COFFEE WITH CREAM

After a lazy alfresco brunch, what could be nicer than this cool, sophisticated iced coffee?

INGREDIENTS

1 ¾ cups water

2 tbsp instant coffee granules

2 tbsp brown sugar

6 ice cubes, crushed

light cream

whole coffee beans

SERVES 2

Use the water and coffee granules to brew some hot coffee, then let cool to room temperature. Transfer to a pitcher, then cover with plastic wrap and chill in the refrigerator for at least 45 minutes.

When the coffee has chilled, pour it into a food processor. Add the sugar and process until well combined. Add the ice cubes and process until smooth.

Pour the mixture into glasses. Float light cream on the top, then decorate with whole coffee beans and serve.

BUCK'S FIZZ

INGREDIENTS

2 measures orange juice, chilled

2 measures champagne, chilled

SERVES 1

Half fill a chilled flute with orange juice then gently pour in the chilled champagne.

Invented at Buck's Club in London, the original was invariably made with Bollinger champagne and it is true that the better the quality of the champagne, the better the flavor.

MIMOSA

So called because it resembles the color of a mimosa's attractive
yellow bloom.

INGREDIENTS
juice of 1 passion fruit

½ measure orange Curaçao

crushed ice

champagne, chilled

slice of carambola and twist of citrus peel

SERVES 1
Scoop out the passion fruit flesh into a pitcher or shaker and stir or shake
with the Curaçao and a little crushed ice until frosted.

Pour into the base of a champagne glass and top up with champagne.

Dress with fruit.

SCREWDRIVER

INGREDIENTS

cracked ice cubes

2 measures vodka

orange juice

slice of orange

SERVES 1

Fill a chilled glass with cracked ice cubes. Pour the vodka over the ice and top up with orange juice. Stir well to mix and dress with a slice of orange.

Always use freshly squeezed orange juice to make this refreshing cocktail—it is just not the same with bottled juice. This simple, classic cocktail has given rise to numerous and increasingly elaborate variations.

MINT JULEP

A julep is simply a mixed drink sweetened with syrup. The mint julep was probably first made in the United States, and is the traditional drink of the Kentucky Derby.

INGREDIENTS

leaves from 1 fresh mint sprig

1 tbsp sugar syrup

crushed ice cubes

3 measures bourbon whiskey

fresh mint sprig, to dress

SERVE 1

Put the mint leaves and sugar syrup into a small chilled glass and mash with a teaspoon. Add crushed ice to fill the tumbler, then add the bourbon. Decorate with the mint sprig.

SANGRIA

INGREDIENTS

juice of 1 orange

juice of 1 lemon

2 tbsp powdered sugar

ice

1 orange, thinly sliced

1 lemon, thinly sliced

1 bottle red wine, chilled

lemonade

SERVES 6

Stir the orange and lemon juices with the sugar in a large bowl or pitcher. When the sugar has dissolved, add a few cubes of ice along with the sliced fruit and the wine. Marinate for 1 hour if possible, then add lemonade to taste, along with more ice to serve.

A perfect long, cold, drink for a crowd of friends at a summer brunch.

SEABREEZE

Pink grapefruit juice is much sweeter and subtler than its paler cousin, so it is ideal to mix in cocktails where you want just a slight sharpness.

INGREDIENTS

1½ measures vodka

½ measure cranberry juice

ice

pink grapefruit juice to taste

SERVES 1

Shake the vodka and cranberry juice over ice until frosted. Pour into a chilled tumbler or long glass and top up with grapefruit juice to taste. Serve with a straw.

BELLINI

INGREDIENTS

2 large ripe peaches

1½ cups chilled demi-sec champagne, Moscato di Spumante, or other sparkling white wine

(for a nonalcoholic version use sparkling grape juice)

amaretti cookies, to serve

SERVES 2

Pour boiling water over the peaches to scald them. Drain, then peel and chop them, discarding the pits.

Put the chopped peaches into a food processor and process until smooth.

Divide the peach mixture between 2 champagne flutes. Stir in the champagne or sparkling wine, mixing with a swizzle stick.

Serve at once with a few amaretti cookies.

This is a twist on a classic cocktail. Make sure the champagne or Moscato di Spumante is thoroughly chilled before you begin.

BLOODY MARY

This classic cocktail was invented in 1921 at the legendary Harry's Bar in Paris. There are numerous versions—some much hotter and spicier. Ingredients may include horseradish sauce in addition to, or instead of, Tabasco sauce.

INGREDIENTS

dash of Worcestershire sauce

dash of Tabasco sauce

cracked ice cubes

2 measures vodka

splash dry sherry

6 measures tomato juice

juice ½ lemon

pinch of celery salt

pinch of cayenne pepper

celery stick with leaves

slice of lemon

SERVES 1

Dash the Worcestershire sauce and Tabasco sauce over ice in a shaker and add the vodka, splash of dry sherry, tomato juice, and lemon juice.

Shake vigorously until frosted.

Strain into a tall chilled glass, add a pinch of celery salt, and a pinch of cayenne, and decorate with a celery stick and a slice of lemon.

Sweet Treats

WAFFLES WITH CARAMELIZED BANANAS

Use firm but ripe bananas for this recipe, as softer bananas may disintegrate too easily. Try pears or strawberries for a delicious change.

INGREDIENTS

scant 1¼ cups all-purpose flour

2 tsp baking powder

½ tsp salt

2 tsp superfine sugar

2 eggs, separated

generous 1 cup milk

¾ stick butter, melted

CARAMELIZED BANANAS

7 tbsp butter, cut into pieces

3 tbsp corn syrup

3 large ripe bananas, peeled and thickly sliced

MAKES 12 WAFFLES TO SERVE 4–6

Mix the flour, baking powder, salt, and sugar together in a bowl. Whisk the egg yolks, milk, and melted butter together with a fork, then stir this mixture into the dry ingredients to make a smooth batter.

Using an electric mixer or hand whisk, whisk the egg whites in a clean glass bowl until stiff peaks form. Fold into the batter. Spoon 2 large tablespoons of the batter into a preheated waffle maker and cook according to the manufacturer's instructions.

To make the caramelized bananas, melt the butter with the corn syrup in a pan over low heat and stir until combined. Let simmer for a few minutes until the caramel thickens and darkens slightly. Add the bananas and mix gently to coat. Pour over the warm waffles and serve at once.

FRENCH TOAST WITH MAPLE SYRUP

INGREDIENTS

6 eggs

6 fl oz/175 ml milk

¾ cup milk

¼ tsp ground cinnamon

salt

12 slices day-old challah or plain white bread

about 4 tbsp butter or margarine, plus extra to serve

½ –1 tbsp sunflower or corn oil

warm maple syrup, to serve

SERVES 4–6

Preheat the oven to 275ºF/140ºC. Break the eggs into a large, shallow dish and beat together with the milk, cinnamon, and salt to taste. Add the bread slices and press them down so that they are covered on both sides with the egg mixture. Leave the bread to stand for 1–2 minutes to soak up the egg mixture, turning the slices over once.

Melt half the butter or margarine with ½ tablespoon of oil in a large skillet. Add as many bread slices as will fit in a single layer to the pan and cook for 2–3 minutes until golden brown.

Turn the bread slices over and cook until golden brown on the other side. Transfer the French toast to a plate and keep warm in the oven while cooking the remaining bread slices, adding extra oil if necessary.

Serve the French toast with the remaining butter melting on top and warm maple syrup for pouring over.

Always popular for breakfast or brunch, French toast is the American version of the French pain perdu. The French title translates as "lost bread," referring to the day-old, slightly stale bread that is best to use for this sweet breakfast dish.

DRIED CHERRY CHEESECAKE MUFFINS

The dried cherries are mixed in with the flour to prevent them from sinking to the bottom of the muffins and to ensure that they are evenly distributed. Try the same technique with your favorite fruitcake recipe! Dried cranberries also work well here.

INGREDIENTS

1 stick, plus 3 tbsp butter, plus extra for greasing

scant 1 cup cream cheese

generous ¾ cup superfine sugar

3 large eggs, lightly beaten

2 cups self-rising flour

generous ½ cup dried cherries, chopped

confectioners' sugar, for dusting

MAKES 12 MUFFINS

Preheat the oven to 350°F/180°C. Grease a deep 12-cup muffin pan.

Melt the butter and let cool slightly. In a large bowl, whisk the cream cheese and sugar together, add the eggs one at a time until well combined, and then stir in the melted butter.

Mix the flour and cherries together in a bowl, then stir gently into the batter. Spoon into the prepared muffin pan, filling each hole to about two-thirds full, and bake for 12–15 minutes, or until golden brown. Remove from the oven and let cool on a wire rack. Eat warm or cold, dusted lightly with confectioners' sugar.

BERRY & YOGURT CRUNCH

INGREDIENTS

generous ¾ cup rice, buckwheat, or millet flakes, or a mixture

4 tbsp honey

1 lb 2 oz/500 g thick plain yogurt

finely grated rind of 1 orange

1 cup frozen mixed berries, partially thawed, plus extra to decorate

SERVE 4

Heat a dry skillet over medium heat, add the flakes, and toast, shaking the skillet, for 1 minute. Add half the honey and stir to coat the flakes. Cook, stirring constantly, until the flakes turn golden brown and slightly crisp.

Put the yogurt into a bowl and stir in the remaining honey and the orange rind. Gently stir in the berries, reserving a few to decorate. Let stand for 10–15 minutes for the berries to release their juices, then stir again to give a swirl of color.

To serve, spoon a layer of flakes into the bottoms of four glasses, then top with a layer of the berry yogurt. Sprinkle with another layer of flakes and add another layer of the yogurt. Decorate with the reserved berries.

DOUGHNUT MUFFINS

It is important to brush the warm muffins with melted butter, and sprinkle the cinnamon and sugar mixture over them immediately. If you wait too long, the butter will sink into the muffins and the sugar will not stick.

INGREDIENTS

1½ sticks butter, softened, plus extra for greasing

1 cup superfine sugar

2 large eggs, lightly beaten

generous 2½ cups all-purpose flour

2 tsp baking powder

¼ tsp baking soda

pinch of salt

½ tsp freshly grated nutmeg

generous 1 cup milk

TOPPING

½ cup superfine sugar

1 tsp ground cinnamon

2 tbsp butter, melted

MAKES 12 MUFFINS

Preheat the oven to 350°F/180°C. Grease a deep 12-cup muffin pan.

In a large bowl, beat the butter and sugar together until light and creamy. Add the eggs, a little at a time, beating well between additions.

Sift the flour, baking powder, baking soda, salt, and nutmeg together. Add half to the creamed mixture with half of the milk. Gently fold the ingredients together before incorporating the remaining flour and milk. Spoon the mixture into the prepared muffin pan, filling each hole to about two-thirds full. Bake for 15–20 minutes, or until the muffins are lightly brown and firm to the touch.

For the topping, mix the sugar and cinnamon together. While the muffins are still warm from the oven, brush lightly with melted butter, and sprinkle over the cinnamon and sugar mixture. Eat warm or cold.

BANANA BREAD WITH STRAWBERRY COMPOTE & MASCARPONE

INGREDIENTS

1 stick plus 1 tbsp butter, softened, plus extra for greasing

½ cup superfine sugar

¼ cup brown sugar

3 eggs

1 tsp vanilla extract

3 large, ripe bananas

1⅔ cups self-rising flour

1 tsp freshly grated nutmeg

1 tsp ground cinnamon

confectioners' sugar, sifted, for dusting (optional)

mascarpone cheese or plain yogurt, to serve

STRAWBERRY COMPOTE

scant ½ cup brown sugar

juice of 2 oranges

grated rind of 1 orange

1 cinnamon stick

14 oz/400 g fresh strawberries, hulled and thickly sliced

SERVES 4

Preheat the oven to 350°F/180°C. Grease a 9 x 4¼-inch/23 x 11-cm loaf pan and line the base with nonstick parchment paper.

Put the butter and sugars in a bowl and beat together until light and fluffy. Mix in the eggs, one at a time, then mix in the vanilla extract. Peel the bananas and mash roughly with the back of a fork. Stir gently into the butter mixture, then add the flour, nutmeg, and cinnamon, stirring until just combined.

Pour the mixture into the prepared pan and bake in the preheated oven for 1¼ hours, or until a skewer inserted into the center comes out clean. Let stand in the pan for 5 minutes before turning out onto a wire rack to cool.

To make the compote, put the sugar, orange juice and rind, and cinnamon stick in a pan and bring to a boil. Add the strawberries and return to a boil. Remove from the heat, then pour into a clean heatproof bowl and let cool. Remove the cinnamon stick. Serve slices of the banana bread with a dollop of mascarpone cheese or yogurt and spoon over the warm or cold compote. Dust with sifted confectioners' sugar if desired.

The bread can be stored in the freezer for up to three months. Thaw overnight in the refrigerator before serving. It can also be iced for a delicious treat.

SPICED FRENCH TOAST WITH SEASONAL BERRIES

This oven-baked method of making French toast uses much less fat than the pan-fried version and makes it easy to produce larger quantities.

INGREDIENTS

4 eggs, plus 1 extra egg white

¼ tsp ground cinnamon

¼ tsp allspice

4 slices thick white bread

1 tbsp sweet butter, melted

fresh mint sprigs, to decorate

SEASONAL BERRIES

scant ½ cup superfine sugar

¼ cup freshly squeezed orange juice

10½ oz/300 g mixed fresh seasonal berries, such as strawberries, raspberries, and blueberries, picked over and hulled

SERVES 4

Preheat the oven to 425°F/220°C. Put the eggs and egg white in a large, shallow bowl or dish and whisk together with a fork. Add the cinnamon and allspice, and whisk until combined.

To prepare the berries, put the sugar and orange juice in a pan and bring to a boil over low heat, stirring until the sugar has dissolved. Add the berries, then remove from the heat and let cool for 10 minutes.

Meanwhile, soak the bread slices in the egg mixture for about 1 minute on each side. Brush a large baking sheet with the melted butter and place the bread slices on the sheet. Bake in the preheated oven for 5–7 minutes, or until lightly browned. Turn the slices over and bake for an additional 2–3 minutes. Serve the berries spooned over the toast and decorated with mint sprigs.

SIMPLE CINNAMON ROLLS

INGREDIENTS

scant 2½ cups self-rising flour, plus extra for rolling

pinch of salt

2 tbsp superfine sugar

1 tsp ground cinnamon

7 tbsp butter, melted, plus extra for greasing

2 egg yolks

scant 1 cup milk, plus extra for glazing

FILLING

1 tsp ground cinnamon

generous ¼ cup brown sugar

2 tbsp superfine sugar

1 tbsp butter, melted

FROSTING

generous 1 cup confectioners' sugar, sifted

2 tbsp cream cheese, softened

1 tbsp butter, softened

about 2 tbsp boiling water

1 tsp vanilla extract

MAKES 8 ROLLS

Preheat the oven to 350°F/180°C. Grease an 8-inch/20-cm round pan and line the bottom with parchment paper.

Mix the flour, salt, superfine sugar, and cinnamon together in a bowl. Whisk the butter, egg yolks, and milk together and combine with the dry ingredients to make a soft dough. Turn out onto a large piece of waxed paper, lightly sprinkled with flour, and roll out to a rectangle 12 x 10 inches/30 x 25 cm.

To make the filling, mix the ingredients together, spread evenly over the dough and roll up, jelly-roll style, to form a log. Using a sharp knife, cut the dough into 8 even-size slices and pack into the prepared pan. Brush gently with extra milk and bake for 30–35 minutes, or until golden brown. Remove from the oven and let cool for 5 minutes before removing from the pan.

To make the frosting, sift the confectioners' sugar into a large bowl and make a well in the center. Place the cream cheese and butter in the center, pour over the water, and stir to mix. Add extra boiling water, a few drops at a time, until the frosting coats the back of a spoon. Stir in the vanilla extract. Drizzle over the rolls. Serve warm or cold.

These cinnamon rolls are best eaten warm, on the same day they are made. As a variation, add 2 tablespoons of raisins to the filling and proceed as per the recipe.

APPLE MUESLI

INGREDIENTS

generous ⅓ cup sunflower seeds

scant ¼ cup pepitas

generous ½ cup shelled hazelnuts,
coarsely chopped

generous 1¼ cups buckwheat flakes

generous 1¼ cups rice flakes

¾ cup millet flakes

⅔ cup dried apple, coarsely chopped

⅔ cup dried pitted dates,
coarsely chopped

MAKES 10 PORTIONS

Heat a dry skillet over medium heat, add the seeds and hazelnuts, and lightly toast, shaking the skillet frequently, for 4 minutes, or until golden brown. Transfer to a large mixing bowl and let cool.

Add the flakes, apple, and dates to the bowl and mix thoroughly until combined. Store the muesli in an airtight jar or container.

BLUEBERRY PANCAKES

INGREDIENTS

1 cup all-purpose flour

2 tbsp superfine sugar

2 tbsp baking powder

½ tsp salt

scant 1 cup buttermilk

3 tbsp sweet butter, melted

1 large egg

5 oz/140 g fresh blueberries, plus
extra to serve

sunflower or corn oil, for oiling

butter

warm maple syrup, to serve

MAKES 10–12

Preheat the oven to 275ºF/140ºC. Sift the flour, sugar, baking powder, and salt together into a large bowl and make a well in the center.

Beat the buttermilk, butter, and egg together in a separate small bowl, then pour the mixture into the well in the dry ingredients. Beat the dry ingredients into the liquid, gradually drawing them in from the side, until a smooth batter is formed. Gently stir in the blueberries.

Heat a large skillet over medium-high heat until a splash of water dances on the surface. Using a pastry brush or crumpled piece of paper towel, oil the base of the skillet.

Drop about 4 tablespoons of batter separately into the skillet and spread each out into a 4-inch/10-cm circle. Continue adding as many pancakes as will fit in your skillet. Cook until small bubbles appear on the surface, then flip over with a spatula and cook the pancakes on the other side for an additional 1–2 minutes, or until the bases are golden brown.

Transfer the pancakes to a warmed plate and keep warm in the preheated oven while you cook the remaining batter, lightly oiling the skillet as before. Make a stack of the pancakes with parchment paper in between each pancake.

Serve with a pat of butter on top of each pancake, extra blueberries on the side and warm maple syrup for pouring over.

HOMEMADE GRANOLA

To vary the flavor, try different dried fruits, such as apricots, raisins, or prunes, as well as dried seeds and nuts. As the granola cools, break up any large pieces that have formed with your hands.

INGREDIENTS

generous 2¾ cups rolled oats

2 Granny Smith or similar tart apples, peeled and diced

scant ⅔ cup dried figs, chopped

½ cup slivered almonds

2 tbsp honey

¼ cup cold water

1 tsp ground cinnamon

1 tsp vanilla extract

1 tsp butter, melted, for greasing

plain yogurt, to serve

SERVES 6−8

Preheat the oven to 325°F/160°C. Mix the oats, apples, figs, and almonds together in a large bowl. Bring the honey, water, cinnamon, and vanilla extract to a boil in a pan, then pour over the oat mixture, stirring well to make sure that all the ingredients are coated.

Lightly grease a large baking sheet with the butter and spread the oat mixture out evenly on the sheet. Bake for 40–45 minutes, or until the granola is golden brown, stirring with a fork from time to time to break up any lumps. Pour onto a clean baking sheet and let cool before storing in an airtight container. Serve sprinkled over bowls of fresh plain yogurt.

CITRUS FRUIT & GINGER COMPOTE

INGREDIENTS

4 oranges

1 lemongrass stalk

⅔ cup freshly squeezed orange juice

½-inch/1-cm piece fresh ginger root, peeled and sliced

4 cardamom pods, lightly crushed

4 cloves

2 tbsp honey

4 tbsp plain yogurt

1 tbsp slivered almonds, toasted

SERVES 4

Peel the oranges, cut into thick slices, and place in a bowl. Trim the lemongrass to retain the bottom third or white part of the stalk. Peel away the outer layers, retaining the tender center, and dice finely.

Combine the orange juice, ginger, cardamom pods, cloves, diced lemongrass, and honey in a pan and bring to a boil. Let simmer for 1 minute, then let cool.

When cool, strain the mixture over the sliced oranges, cover, and let chill in the refrigerator for 1 hour or overnight. Serve in individual dishes with a spoonful of yogurt and a sprinkling of toasted slivered almonds.

Lemongrass is a available in some large supermarkets and Asian markets . If you have trouble finding it, use some very finely grated lemon rind instead.

FRUIT MUFFINS

If you like dried figs, they make a deliciously crunchy alternative to the apricots; they also go very well with the flavor of orange. Other dried fruit, finely chopped, can be used as well.

INGREDIENTS

2 cups self-rising whole-wheat flour

2 tsp baking powder

2 tbsp brown sugar

generous ½ cup dried apricots, finely chopped

1 banana, mashed with 1 tbsp orange juice

1 tsp finely grated orange rind

1¼ cups skim milk

1 large egg, beaten

3 tbsp sunflower or peanut oil

2 tbsp rolled oats

fruit spread, honey, or maple syrup, to serve

MAKES 10

Preheat the oven to 400°F/200°C. Line 10 cups of a 12-cup muffin pan with muffin paper liners. Sift the flour and baking powder into a mixing bowl, adding any husks that remain in the strainer. Stir in the sugar and chopped apricots.

Make a well in the center and add the mashed banana, orange rind, milk, beaten egg, and oil. Mix together well to form a thick batter and divide evenly among the muffin liners.

Sprinkle with a few rolled oats and bake in the oven for 25–30 minutes until well risen and firm to the touch, or until a toothpick inserted into the center comes out clean.

Remove the muffins from the oven and place them on a cooling rack to cool slightly. Serve the muffins while still warm with a little fruit spread, honey, or maple syrup.

GOOSEBERRY FOOL

INGREDIENTS

1 lb 9 oz/700 g fresh gooseberries

generous ½ cup superfine sugar

3 tbsp elderflower cordial

1¼ cups heavy cream

lemon balm or mint leaves, to decorate

crisp cookies or sponge fingers, to serve

SERVES 6

Trim the gooseberries and put in a pan with the sugar. Cook over low heat, stirring constantly, until the fruit is softened to a pulp.

Remove from the heat and beat well with a wooden spoon until you have a thick purée. If you would like a smoother consistency, use the back of a wooden spoon to press the purée through a nylon strainer into a bowl to remove the seeds. Stir in the elderflower cordial. Taste for sweetness at this point and add a little more sugar if needed. Let cool.

Whip the cream in a bowl until it is thick but not too dry. Using a metal spoon, gently fold in the cold gooseberry purée until only just combined—the fool looks more attractive if it has a marbled appearance.

Spoon into six glass serving dishes or a large glass bowl, then cover with plastic wrap and chill well in the refrigerator. Decorate with lemon balm or mint leaves, and serve with crisp cookies or sponge fingers.

GRANOLA BARS

These bars can be stored in an airtight container for up to
3–4 days. Honey can be used in place of the corn syrup for a slightly
less sweet version.

INGREDIENTS

2 sticks sweet butter, plus extra for greasing

1 cup light brown sugar

scant $\frac{1}{3}$ cup corn syrup

1 lb/450 g rolled oats

2 tsp ground cinnamon

4 oz/115 g dried berries, such as cranberries
and blueberries

MAKES 18

Preheat the oven to 350°F/180°C. Line an 8 x 12-inch/20 x 30-cm deep
baking pan with nonstick parchment paper.

Put the butter, sugar, and syrup in a pan and heat over low heat until melted.

Add the rolled oats and cinnamon and stir well. Add the dried berries and stir
to distribute them evenly throughout the oats.

Pour the mixture into the prepared baking pan, then press down well and
bake in the center of the preheated oven for 30–35 minutes, or until golden-
brown but still moist and slightly soft when pressed.

Remove from the oven and let cool for 5 minutes. Cut into 18 pieces and let
cool completely before removing from the pan.

YOGURT WITH HONEY, NUTS & BLUEBERRIES

INGREDIENTS

3 tbsp honey

scant ¾ cup mixed unsalted nuts

½ cup plain yogurt

scant 1 cup fresh blueberries

SERVES 4

Heat the honey in a small pan over medium heat, add the nuts and stir until they are well coated. Remove from the heat and let cool slightly.

Divide the yogurt among four serving bowls, then spoon over the nut mixture and blueberries.

If you prefer to add more fruit, raspberries or strawberries would make a colorful addition.

BILBERRY BIRCHER MUESLI

If bilberries or blueberries are unavailable, substitute any other fresh berries. Add a sliced banana for a more substantial snack.

INGREDIENTS

generous 1 cup rolled oats

generous ¾ cup apple juice

1 red apple, cored

1 tbsp lemon juice

scant ¼ cup chopped toasted hazelnuts

½ tsp ground cinnamon

scant ½ cup plain yogurt

2 tbsp clear honey (optional)

2½ oz/70 g fresh bilberries or blueberries

SERVES 1

Put the oats and apple juice in a bowl, then cover with plastic wrap and let soak in the refrigerator for an hour, or overnight.

Grate or chop the apple and mix with the lemon juice to prevent the fruit from browning. Add the apple, hazelnuts, and cinnamon to the oat mixture and mix well. Spoon the mixture into serving bowls and top with the yogurt. Drizzle over the honey, if using. Spoon the bilberries over the muesli and serve.

NUTTY CEREAL

INGREDIENTS

generous ¾ cup shelled pecans, chopped

scant 1 cup shelled hazelnuts, chopped

1 cup slivered almonds

⅔ cup dried apricots

⅜ cup sunflower seeds

1¼ cups rolled oats

freshly sliced banana

strawberries or raspberries

milk, to serve

SERVES 6

Preheat the oven to 375°F/190°C. Spread all the nuts out on a baking sheet and toast in the preheated oven for 12–15 minutes, turning occasionally. Remove from the oven and let cool.

Meanwhile, finely chop the apricots. Put the cooled nuts, apricots, seeds, and oats into a large mixing bowl and mix together. Store in an airtight container.

When ready to serve, spoon 2–3 tablespoons into separate serving bowls, top with sliced banana, and a few strawberries or raspberries, then pour over a little milk and serve.

CHOCOLATE CRÊPES WITH BERRY COMPOTE

For a more indulgent treat, serve with hot chocolate sauce made by melting 4 squares bittersweet chocolate with 1/2 cup heavy cream.

INGREDIENTS

generous ⅔ cup all-purpose flour

scant ¼ cup unsweetened cocoa

pinch of salt

1 egg

2 tbsp superfine sugar

1½ cups milk

scant 2 tbsp sweet butter

confectioners' sugar, for dusting

ice cream or heavy cream, to serve

BERRY COMPOTE

5½ oz/150 g fresh blackberries

5½ oz/150 g fresh blueberries

8 oz/225 g fresh raspberries

generous ¼ cup superfine sugar

juice of ½ lemon

½ tsp allspice (optional)

MAKES 8–10

Preheat the oven to 275°F/140°C. Sift the flour, unsweetened cocoa, and salt together into a large bowl and make a well in the center.

Beat the egg, sugar, and half the milk together in a separate bowl, then pour the mixture into the dry ingredients. Beat the dry ingredients into the liquid, gradually drawing them in from the side, until a batter is formed. Gradually beat in the remaining milk. Pour the batter into a pitcher.

Heat a 7-inch/18-cm nonstick skillet over medium heat and add 1 teaspoon of the butter. When the butter has melted, pour in enough batter just to cover the bottom, then swirl it round the skillet while tilting it so that you have a thin, even layer. Cook for 30 seconds and then lift up the edge of the crêpe to check if it is cooked. Loosen the crêpe around the edge, then flip it over with a spatula or palette knife. Alternatively, toss the crêpe by flipping the skillet quickly with a flick of the wrist and catching it carefully. Cook on the other side until the bottom is golden brown.

Transfer the crêpe to a warmed plate and keep warm in the preheated oven while you cook the remaining batter, adding the remaining butter to the skillet as necessary. Make a stack of the crêpes with parchment paper in between each crêpe.

To make the compote, pick over the berries and put in a pan with the sugar, lemon juice, and allspice, if using. Cook over low heat until the sugar has dissolved and the berries are warmed through. Do not overcook. Put a crêpe on a warmed serving plate and spoon some of the compote onto the center. Either roll or fold the crêpe and dust with confectioners' sugar. Repeat with the remaining crêpes. Serve with ice cream or heavy cream.

index